Building a
community
of readers

Book-Rich
Environments
Initiative

ALLEN COUNTY
PUBLIC LIBRARY

FORT WAYNE housing authority

D1414648

Albert Einstein

Copyright © 2015 by Quelle Histoire / quellehistoire.com
Published by Roaring Brook Press
Roaring Brook Press is a division of Holtzbrinck Publishing Holdings Limited Partnership
175 Fifth Avenue, New York, NY 10010
mackids.com
All rights reserved

Library of Congress Control Number: 2017957498
ISBN 978-1-250-16609-8

Our books may be purchased in bulk for promotional, educational, or business use.
Please contact your local bookseller or the Macmillan Corporate and Premium Sales Department
at (800) 221-7945 ext. 5442 or by e-mail at MacmillanSpecialMarkets@macmillan.com.

First published in France in 2015 by Quelle Histoire, Paris
First U.S. edition, 2018

Text: Patricia Crété
Translation: Catherine Nolan
Illustrations: Bruno Wennagel, Mathieu Ferret, Guillaume Biasse, Aurélie Verdon

Printed in China by RR Donnelley Asia Printing Solutions Ltd., Dongguan City, Guangdong Province
10 9 8 7 6 5 4 3 2 1

Albert Einstein

Roaring Brook Press
New York

Daydreamer

Albert Einstein was a genius. But he didn't seem like one when he was a boy.

Albert was born in Germany in 1879. He grew up in the city of Munich.

Albert struggled in school. He didn't listen in class. He didn't do his homework. Instead, he daydreamed.

———

1879

Switzerland

Albert's parents didn't know what to do with him. When he turned sixteen, they sent him to a school in Switzerland.

It was a whole new kind of learning for Albert. Instead of memorizing facts, he was allowed to think for himself. He loved it!

Albert began to shine, especially in math and science.

1895

The Equation

After Albert finished school, he took a job at an office. He got married and had two children.

All the while, Albert kept studying science. In 1905, he came up with an equation: $E=mc^2$.

The equation was about energy and the speed of light. Most people didn't understand it! But scientists saw that it was brilliant.

———

1900–1905

Nobel Prize

Albert came up with more amazing ideas. In 1916, he wrote a paper about them. Scientists read Albert's paper and did experiments. They proved that Albert's ideas were right!

In 1921, Albert won the Nobel Prize in Physics, the biggest award in his field.

By now Albert was very famous, but he still enjoyed doing the same things as always: reading, studying, and sailing on the lake near his home.

_____

1914–1921

Politics

Because Albert was so well-known around the world, people listened to his ideas—not just about science but about politics, too.

Albert was Jewish, and he supported making a homeland for the Jews. Much later, after Israel was formed, he was asked to be its president! He politely refused.

Albert was invited to work with the League of Nations, a group that sought peace in Europe. Today, that group is called the United Nations.

———

1919–1952

America

By the 1930s, war was brewing in Europe. A cruel leader named Adolf Hitler wanted to oppress and kill Jewish people.

Albert's life was in danger if he stayed in Europe. He decided to move to the United States.

1933

The Bomb

Albert settled in New Jersey and became a college professor.

In 1939, Albert found out that scientists in Europe were trying to build a very dangerous kind of bomb for Hitler. He wrote a letter to President Roosevelt, warning about it.

The president took Albert's letter seriously. He told American scientists to build the same kind of bomb. The scientists used some of Albert's ideas to make it.

In 1945, the United States dropped the bomb on areas in Japan. Albert was horrified when he saw the destruction it caused.

_____

1939–1945

Civil Rights

Albert stayed in the United States after the war ended. At that time in America, black people did not have the same rights as white people. Albert knew that was wrong.

"I do not intend to be quiet about it," he said. Albert joined the civil rights movement. He made speeches, arguing for equal rights for everyone.

——

1946

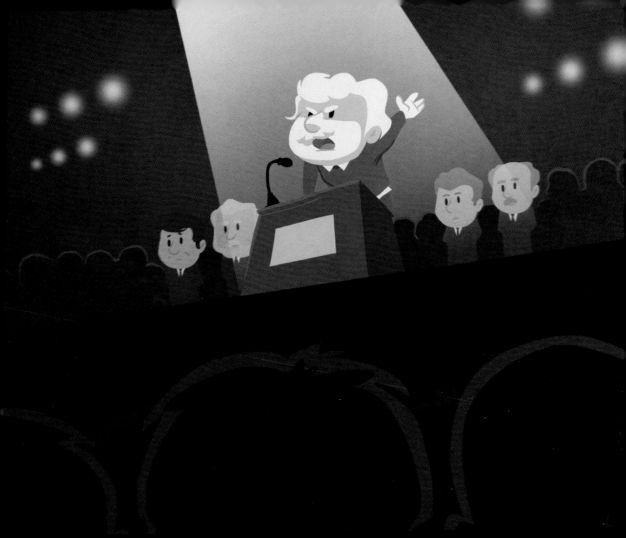

Later Years

Albert kept speaking out about issues his whole life. Some of his views were popular, but some of them weren't. The American government didn't trust Albert, so they watched him secretly.

As he got older, Albert's hair turned white. It stuck out all over his head. When people think of him today, they often remember his wild hair.

———

1937–1949

Genius

Albert died on April 18, 1955. He was seventy-six years old.

He's still called one of the smartest people who ever lived.

———

1955

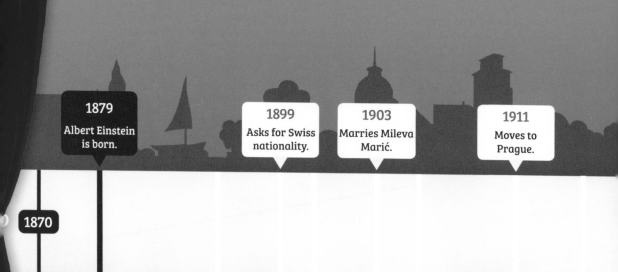

1879
Albert Einstein is born.

1899
Asks for Swiss nationality.

1903
Marries Mileva Marić.

1911
Moves to Prague.

1870

1895
Goes to school in Switzerland.

1901
Publishes his first scientific article.

1905
Comes up with his famous equation.

1914
Moves to Berlin.

1921
Wins the
Nobel Prize.

1928
Joins the board
of the League
for Human
Rights.

1939
Writes to
President
Roosevelt
about the
bomb.

1955
Dies at age
seventy-six.

1960

1923
Visits
Palestine.

1933
Moves to the
United States.

1952
Turns down
an offer to be
president of
Israel.

Europe

1 Munich

Albert spent his childhood here.

2 Zurich

Albert went to school in this Swiss city.

3 Bern

Albert lived here with his family from 1903 to 1905. His apartment is now a museum.

4 Berlin

This city is the capital of Germany.

5 Antwerp

Albert sailed to America from this port in Belgium.

6 Paris

This was the host city for the League for Human Rights. Albert worked with this group.

 France

 Belgium

 Germany

 Switzerland

People to Know

Hermann Einstein
(1847–1902)
Albert's father owned a small company.
He encouraged his son to be a freethinker.

Marcel Grossmann
(1878–1936)
This classmate of Albert's became good
friends with Albert and his wife, Mileva.
Marcel helped Albert get a job in Bern.

Paul Robeson
(1898–1976)
This American singer and actor fought
for equal rights in America.
Albert supported his work.

Bertrand Russell
(1872–1970)
Albert met Bertrand, a British
mathematician, in the United States.
Both men were pacifists.

....

One of the schools Albert
went to as a boy is now
named after him.

....

Albert's brain was stolen after he
died! His doctor, Thomas Harvey,
wanted to study it.

....

Albert was a pacifist. That meant he didn't believe in war. Yet his ideas helped create the world's first nuclear bomb.

....

Albert played the violin and the piano.

Available Now

 Muhammad Ali

 Neil Armstrong

 Blackbeard

 Coco Chanel

 Charlie Chaplin

 Cleopatra

 Marie Curie

 Albert Einstein

 Abraham Lincoln

 Nelson Mandela

 Isaac Newton

 Rosa Parks

Coming Soon

 Anne Frank

 Gandhi

 Frida Kahlo

 Martin Luther King, Jr.